Elevate
YOUR GREATNESS

CHOOSE JOY, REWIRE YOUR LIFE, AND
BUILD A FULFILLING FUTURE

Melissa Dotson

©Copyright 2025, Melissa Dotson.
All rights reserved.

No portion of this book may be reproduced by mechanical, photographic, or electronic process; nor may it be stored in a retrieval system, transmitted in any form, or otherwise be copied for public use or private use without written permission of the copyright owner.

Although the publisher and the author have made every effort to ensure that the information in this book was correct at press time and while this publication is designed to provide accurate information in regard to the subject matter covered, the publisher and the author assume no responsibility for errors, inaccuracies, omissions, or any other inconsistencies herein and hereby disclaim any liability to any party for any loss, damage, or disruption caused by errors or omissions, whether such errors or omissions result from negligence, accident, or any other cause.

This work is solely the author's opinion and not intended to damage the reputation of anyone. It is with the intention to gain a behind the scenes perspective, educate and inspire.

It is sold with the understanding that the publisher and the individual authors are not engaged in the rendering of psychological, legal, accounting, or other professional advice. The content and views in each chapter are the sole expression and opinion of its author and not necessarily the views of Fig Factor Media, LLC.

For More Information:
Fig Factor Media | figfactormedia.com
Melissa Dotson | melissaAdotson.com

Cover Design by DG Marco Antonio Álvarez Rodríguez
Layout by LDG Juan Manuel Serna Rosales

Printed in the United States of America

ISBN: 978-1-961600-56-0
Library of Congress Control Number: 2025909096

Dedication

To my family, friends, and all my teachers, mentors, and coaches along the way.

This book is also dedicated to anyone who has at least one area in their life that they want to improve.

Table of Contents

Acknowledgments 5
Introduction 6

    Personal Fulfillment Is an Inside Job 9
    The Time Is Now—What Are You Waiting For? 17
    The Change Formula: Why People Don't Change 23
    Energy Leaks: Protecting Your Most Valuable Resource 29
    How Do You Want to Show Up in the World? 43
    What Really Matters? Only You Know 51
    You Already Have the Power 61
    Creating Space for the Life You Want 69
    The Power of Focus: Do Less, Achieve More 85
    Energy Flow: Working with Your Natural Rhythm 93
    Giving from Abundance: The Art of True Generosity 103
    You Find What You're Looking for 107
    This Isn't the End—It's Just the Beginning 113

Bibliography 116
About the Author 117

Acknowledgments

This book would not have been possible without the incredible team at Rieke Interiors. Your dedication, leadership, and commitment to excellence in the day-to-day allowed me the space and clarity to pour myself into this project. I'm deeply grateful for your support, your trust, and the way you've continued to perform your work with such reliability and excellence.

Creating this book has been a joyful and fulfilling journey. My hope is that within these pages, at least one *"aha"* moment finds its way to your heart—and maybe even lights the spark for lasting change.

Introduction

For over 20 years, I've immersed myself in the world of personal development—researching, practicing, reading, listening, and absorbing everything I could. Along the way, I discovered something both simple and profound: living an elevated, personally fulfilled life comes down to one thing—living consciously. It means being present to what truly matters to you and taking the next right step from that place of awareness.

This book is my way of sharing the most meaningful lessons, tools, and insights I've gathered over the years. Inside, you'll find not just reflections and stories, but interactive exercises designed to help you reconnect with yourself, clarify what matters most, and move forward in alignment with your values.

It's not a formula—it's a framework to help you create a life that feels free, full, and unapologetically yours.

Why listen to me? I am still in the thick of it with much more room to learn. My purpose on earth is to be an uplifter and inspire others to live their life with the most joy and love they can. I hope I inspire you to try some of the things in this book and I hope you get at least one "aha" that you are willing to share with your people and on my website. I don't want you to take what I say at face value, I want you to try the tools in this book for yourself, prove me right or wrong.

Remember there are ebbs and flows in life, just because something didn't work the first time doesn't mean it won't work in the future if you try it again. We are constantly changing beings. Our body constantly renews itself at varying rates, with some cells, like skin and gut, replacing every few days. Others, like red blood cells, every few months. Because we're constantly changing—physically, mentally, and emotionally—what doesn't work for us today might be exactly what we need tomorrow.

Use what works for you and leave the rest. It is like trying on clothes, just because you try them on, doesn't mean you have to buy them. Every personal growth journey begins from a different place—and that's what makes it yours.

In life you find what you're looking for. My motto is "everything always works out for me." So, when I'm looking for that, that is what I get—things working out for me.

I am truly passionate about people living their best life. I have devoted a lot of time to my employees, children, and friends, pushing them to look at things differently and trying to figure out what really matters to them. When I hear about people having "aha" moments I get just as excited as if it were happening to me.

The definition of an "aha moment": a powerful moment of realization that sparks clarity, joy, or a sense of triumph.

Think of this book as your personal coach. Start wherever you are—there's no need to read cover to cover in order. Begin with the chapter that speaks to you most and go from there. Each section stands on its own and includes practical exercises designed to help you apply the insights directly to your everyday life. This is your journey—move through it in the way that feels most aligned to you. However, I challenge you to do all the exercises.

My wish for you is to feel spontaneous moments of joy coming from your insides, not external things.

Now, let's begin your personal journey—one step, one insight, one breakthrough at a time.

PERSONAL FULFILLMENT IS AN INSIDE JOB

Within the quiet chambers of your soul lies joy no world can give or take away.

For much of life, we are taught to focus on building the outside world—getting an education, securing a good job, buying a home, and perhaps starting a family. These milestones create a sense of accomplishment, but they often come with the illusion that external success will bring lasting happiness.

In reality, these achievements offer temporary bursts of joy. A new promotion, a dream vacation, or a big purchase might bring excitement, but the feeling fades. This is because external rewards trigger short-lived dopamine spikes, not deep, lasting fulfillment. The cycle continues—chasing the next milestone, seeking the next high, always believing that something *out there* will finally make us feel complete.

But real, sustainable joy comes from within. When you shift your focus inward—cultivating self-awareness, emotional resilience, and inner peace—you unlock a wellspring of happiness that isn't dependent on circumstances. You start experiencing spontaneous moments of pure joy, like singing in the kitchen, dancing in the car, or feeling at peace for no reason at all. You realize that happiness isn't something to chase; being happy is something to *become*.

When you nurture your inner world, the outside world naturally begins to reflect your inner joy. True fulfillment isn't something you find; it's something you create from within.

Personal fulfillment is the soil, joy is the flower. Fulfillment is the deep-rooted sense that your life aligns with your values, passions, and purpose. It's the quiet knowing that you are on the right path, doing what matters, becoming who you were meant to be.

Joy is the emotional expression of that fulfillment. It's the natural byproduct that bubbles up when your life is in alignment. When you're fulfilled, you don't need a reason to feel good, you just do. You find yourself smiling in the middle of ordinary moments. Laughing more. Feeling lighter. That's joy.

In this way, joy is what fulfillment feels like. And fulfillment is what creates sustainable, grounded joy. They are not separate things you chase. One leads to the other—inner alignment (fulfillment) gives birth to emotional aliveness (joy).

EXERCISE: TURNING INWARD FOR LASTING JOY

Objective: Shift your focus from external achievements to inner fulfillment and experience joy without external triggers.

Step 1: Reflect on Your External Pursuits

Take a few minutes to write down the biggest achievements or milestones you've accomplished so far in life (e.g., job, house, relationships, material success). Next to each, write:

- Did this bring me lasting joy or a temporary high?
- How long did the happiness from this achievement last?
- What did I chase next after that feeling faded?

Step 2: Identify Moments of Inner Joy

Think about a time when you felt pure joy with no external reason, maybe you caught yourself humming while cooking, felt peaceful on a quiet morning, or laughed for no reason at all.

- What were you doing?
- What did that moment feel like?
- How can you invite more of these moments into your daily life?

Step 3: Start a Joy-For-No-Reason Challenge

For the next 7 days, commit to finding one moment of joy each day without relying on external triggers. Some ideas:

- Put on music and dance, just because.
- Close your eyes and take five deep breaths, simply appreciating the moment.
- Step outside and soak in the feeling of the sun or fresh air.
- Smile at yourself in the mirror and say something kind.

Step 4: Reflect on the Experience

At the end of the week, ask yourself:

- Did I feel more joyful without chasing external rewards?
- How did my mood or perspective shift?
- What small habits can I keep to nurture my inner fulfillment?

Contrary to what many believe, our brains are not fixed; they are dynamic and adaptable. Thanks to neuroplasticity, the brain has the remarkable ability to rewire itself based on our thoughts, habits, and experiences. Studies show that consistently practicing positive thinking and gratitude can literally reshape our neural pathways, making joy a more natural and automatic state over time. An article published in the Review of General Psychology revealed that happiness is made up of 50% genetics, 40% intentional activities, and only 10% life circumstances. That means the majority of our joy is within our control. It comes from how we choose to live each day. The more we train our minds toward joy, the more our brains begin to default to happiness.

Our sense of well-being is also deeply connected to our body's own chemistry. Inside us we have built-in happiness chemicals—dopamine, serotonin, and oxytocin. Dopamine fuels motivation and pleasure released when we achieve goals or experience something enjoyable. Serotonin helps stabilize mood and is increased through meditation, sunlight, and gratitude. Oxytocin, often called the "love hormone," is released through acts of kindness, touch, and connection. When we participate in activities like exercise, meaningful conversations, meditation, or helping others, we naturally boost these feel-good chemicals, leading to greater emotional balance and joy.

Another powerful tool for cultivating happiness is mindfulness. Research from the University of California shows that people who regularly practice mindfulness report higher levels of happiness and lower levels of stress. Mindfulness keeps us anchored in the present moment, allowing us to enjoy life as it's happening rather than constantly seeking external validation or worrying about what's next. Interestingly, studies also reveal that when our minds wander they tend to drift toward negative thoughts. Being fully present can help us break that pattern and reconnect with gratitude and joy for what we already have.

Our perspective also plays a critical role in how we experience life. Research in Cognitive Behavioral Therapy (CBT) proves that our thoughts directly shape our emotions. By intentionally choosing positive interpretations of events—especially challenging ones—we can shift from stress and frustration to resilience and happiness. Even something as simple as smiling (yes, even a fake one!) has been shown to stimulate endorphins, tricking the brain into feeling better. This reinforces the idea that joy isn't something we wait for, it's something we create from within.

Finally, joy thrives in meaning and purpose. According to self-determination theory, lasting fulfillment is built on three key human needs: autonomy (feeling in control of your life), competence (the desire to grow and feel capable), and connection (deep, meaningful relationships). Studies confirm that happiness isn't about wealth or achievements, it's about how aligned we are with these inner needs. When we cultivate purpose, nurture personal growth, and invest in our relationships, we create a wellspring of joy that's resilient, authentic, and deeply fulfilling.

Science confirms that joy isn't something external that we find—it's something we create by how we think, what we focus on, and how we engage with life. Our brains are designed to experience joy, and we have the tools within us to activate it every day.

PERSONAL STORY

An example of me learning this powerful lesson came as I was standing on a beautiful beach in Hawaii. We took a family vacation to celebrate the end of my chemo treatment. It should have been a perfect moment. But as I stood there on the phone talking with a friend, venting about feeling irritated with my family and how we just weren't in sync that day, something hit me. Despite the stunning view and the significance of the occasion, I felt disconnected. In that moment, I realized I had felt more genuine joy in my car on a random weekday—singing at the top of my lungs, dancing behind the wheel, completely alone—than I did standing on that beach, which is normally one of my favorite places to be. That moment taught me something profound: inner joy doesn't require an expensive vacation or perfect conditions. Sometimes, all it takes is a shift in perspective and a willingness to find joy in the ordinary.

JOURNAL PROMPT

Reflect and answer the question below.

If I had nothing to prove and no external expectations, what would fulfillment look like for me?

_____
_____
_____
_____
_____

THE TIME IS NOW— WHAT ARE YOU WAITING FOR?

The sun doesn't wait to rise—why should you? Growth happens in cycles, but every moment is an opportunity to begin.

What's your favorite season of the year? The warmth of summer, the crisp air of fall, the renewal of spring, or the stillness of winter?

Now, consider this: if you live to be 80, you only get 80 of those seasons. That's it.

How many have you already lived? How many are left? What are you going to do with them?

Many people wait—for the perfect timing, the right opportunity, or a moment when life magically aligns. But the truth is, that moment will never come. The timing will never be perfect. Waiting for perfection is just another way of avoiding action.

But here's the secret: baby steps will always take you further than waiting for the "right" time. One step today, followed by another tomorrow, will get you where you want to go far more effectively than one big push followed by months of hesitation. Lasting change is built on small, consistent actions—not dramatic, one-time efforts.

We often live in reaction mode, responding to life's challenges instead of proactively creating the life we want. Don't wait until a crisis forces you to change—whether it's illness, job loss, or the passing of someone important to you. Start now, while you have the choice.

EXERCISE: THE "NO-LIMITS DREAM LIST"

(Not a bucket list—this is bigger.)

1. **Imagine there are no barriers.**
   - No fear.
   - No financial limits.
   - No time constraints.
   - No excuses.
   - Just pure possibility.

2. **Write down everything you'd love to experience or do in your lifetime.**
   - What excites you?

   _____
   _____
   _____

   - What have you always wanted to try but never dared?

   _____
   _____
   _____

   - What aligns with your values and the life you truly want?

   _____
   _____
   _____

3. **Pick one thing and take a baby step toward it this week.**
    - If you want to travel, research a destination.
    - If you want to write a book, outline a chapter.
    - If you want to start a business, draft a simple plan.

    The time is now. Your seasons are passing. What will you do with the ones you have left?

    _____
    _____
    _____
    _____
    _____
    _____
    _____
    _____
    _____
    _____
    _____
    _____
    _____
    _____
    _____
    _____

JOURNAL PROMPT

List the obstacles keeping you from taking action now—and how you can break through them.

PERSONAL STORY

My time is now. I had been putting off writing this book for years, now I am doing it. I wrote the book, created the personal branding website, and prepared the speaking content. Now I am sharing my stories and inspiring people to take action. Was I afraid? Yes, I still am. However, I am not going to let that stop me from fulfilling my purpose of teaching how important personal fulfillment is and helping people achieve "aha" moments.

Abraham-Hicks said it best:

> "A happy life is just a string of happy moments. But most people don't allow the happy moment, because they're so busy trying to get a happy life."

Stop waiting for some future moment to feel fulfilled and make it happen now.

THE CHANGE FORMULA: WHY PEOPLE DON'T CHANGE

A caterpillar resists transformation before becoming a butterfly. Change feels uncomfortable, but it leads to something beautiful.

Change is hard. If it weren't, everyone would be effortlessly fit, financially free, deeply fulfilled, and living their best life. But most people struggle to make lasting changes, and there's a reason for that.

Change follows a formula:

D × V × FS > RC

(Dissatisfaction × Vision × First Steps) must be greater than Resistance to Change)

This formula, created by David Gleicher and published by Richard Beckhard in his book *Organizational Transitions* explains why some changes succeed while others fail. If your dissatisfaction with your current situation, your vision for a better future, and your first steps toward that future aren't strong enough to outweigh your resistance, change won't happen.

Let's take a common example: exercising regularly and run it through the change formula, unsuccessfully and successfully.

Imagine someone who wants to work out but can't seem to make it stick.

Change Fails (D × V × FS < RC)

- **D (Dissatisfaction):** Low. They feel a little sluggish but nothing severe. No major health issues yet.

- **V (Vision):** Weak. They think, *"I should exercise,"* but don't have a vivid, inspiring picture of why it matters.

- **FS (First Steps):** Unclear. They don't know where to start or what workout to do.

- **RC (Resistance to Change):** High. They feel tired, intimidated by the gym, and "too busy" to commit.

Result? They skip workouts, fall into old habits, and stay stuck.

How to Make Change Stick (D × V × FS > RC)

1. Increase Dissatisfaction (D)

- Track daily energy levels to see how inactivity makes them feel.
- Get a health check-up to understand risks.
- Try a challenge (e.g., running up stairs) to feel their lack of fitness firsthand.

2. Strengthen Vision (V)

- Imagine their future self: strong, energized, confident.
- Picture playing with their kids without getting winded or fitting into their favorite clothes.
- Follow inspiring fitness transformations.

3. Clarify First Steps (FS)

- Commit to a tiny, easy action: *"I will walk for 10 minutes before work."*
- Set a schedule and treat workouts like brushing their teeth—non-negotiable.
- Get a workout buddy for accountability.

4. Reduce Resistance to Change (RC)

- Make it convenient: Lay out clothes the night before. Choose a nearby gym.
- Make it fun: Dance, hike, swim—don't force something they hate.
- Attach it to a reward: Only listen to a favorite podcast while working out.

Result? They build momentum, see progress, and the habit sticks.

WHY YOU STRUGGLE TO CHANGE

If you keep saying you want to change something but never do, it's because your D × V × FS isn't greater than RC.

To find out what's holding you back, listen to yourself:

- What do you say over and over that you want to change?
- Ask friends or family—they may notice patterns you don't.
- If you're not taking action, ask yourself: *Am I dissatisfied enough? Do I have a clear vision? Do I know my first step?*

Roadblocks to Change: What to Watch For

Change is never a straight line. One of the most common roadblocks is what's known as the J-curve of change—things often get harder before they get better. In the beginning, you might feel like you're slipping backward or losing momentum, but this is exactly when transformation is starting to take root. Don't stop when it gets uncomfortable—that's the moment real growth is happening.

Another challenge comes from the people around you. Not everyone will welcome your growth. Some may prefer the "old you" because it was more convenient or predictable for them. As you evolve, your relationships may shift—and that's okay. It's part of the process. The key is to not let others' discomfort with your progress pull you back into old patterns. Stay focused on the person you're becoming, even if it means outgrowing familiar dynamics along the way.

EXERCISE: MAKE YOUR CHANGE HAPPEN

Step 1: What Do You Want to Change? Write it down. Be specific.

Step 2: Increase Dissatisfaction

- What is frustrating about staying the same?
- How could you make your dissatisfaction even stronger?

Step 3: Strengthen Your Vision

- Close your eyes. Imagine your life after you've made the change.
- What do you see?
- What do you hear?
- What do you feel?
- What does your new life smell like? Taste like? (Example: A healthier you might wake up to the scent of fresh coffee, feeling light and energized.)

Step 4: Take the First Step

- What is one small, easy step you can take today?
- Make it so simple you can't fail.

Step 5: Identify and Overcome Resistance

- What might get in your way? (Time? Fear? Doubt?)
- How will you overcome it? (Set reminders? Get an accountability partner? Make it fun?)

Step 6: Make a Commitment

- Tell someone your first step, when you'll do it, and how.
- Ask them to hold you accountable.

JOURNAL PROMPT

List three fears holding you back and counter them with three empowering truths.

_____
_____
_____
_____
_____
_____
_____
_____
_____
_____
_____
_____

ENERGY LEAKS: PROTECTING YOUR MOST VALUABLE RESOURCE

A leaky dam loses water over time. If you don't seal the cracks (negative habits, distractions, draining people), you'll never build a strong reservoir of energy.

Every day, you wake up with a limited amount of energy, think of it as a fuel tank. How you spend that energy determines the quality of your day, your productivity, and your overall well-being. But energy leaks—unnoticed drains on your mental, emotional, and physical resources—can leave you running on empty.

Common Energy Leaks
- Worry — Playing out worst-case scenarios in your head, most of which never happen.
- Anger and Resentment — Holding onto past hurts instead of letting them go.
- Unspoken Conversations — Holding back what you really need to say weighs you down.
- Doing Things You Dislike — Spending time on things that drain you instead of things that energize you.
- Overcommitment — Saying "yes" when you really mean "no."

If you don't protect your energy, it will get stolen by distractions, unnecessary stress, and things that don't align with what truly matters to you.

ENERGY LEAK: WORRY

Worry is like running a race while sitting in a rocking chair—you feel like you're doing something, but you're going nowhere. It drains your energy without solving anything. And here's the kicker, worrying doesn't prevent bad things from happening. In fact, excessive worry can create a self-fulfilling prophecy by keeping you in a state of stress and inaction.

EXERCISE: THE WORRY LIST

- Write down all your worries. Get them out of your head, heart, and gut.
- Next to each one, ask: "Can I do something about this right now?"

  - If yes → Write down the first step you can take to alleviate this worry.
  - If no → Write *"Let it go."*

This exercise frees up mental energy so you can focus on things that truly matter.

Worry:	Can I do something about it?	First step or let it go:

ENERGY LEAK: ANGER AND RESENTMENT

Emotions are energy in motion. They arrive instantly—in nanoseconds—so you can't control when they show up. What you can control is how you process them.

- Let them move through you instead of stuffing them inside.
- Science says most emotions only last 90 seconds if we don't resist them.
- After they pass, ask yourself: *Why did I feel that way?* The answer may reveal something deeper that needs your attention.

One powerful way to release these emotions is to write them out—completely uncensored. Let it all pour onto the page. Don't worry about how it sounds. In fact, if you feel uncomfortable with anyone else reading it, that's a sign you're doing it right. This exercise isn't for anyone but you. When you're finished, destroy the paper—rip it up, shred it, or safely burn it if that feels right. Let the emotions move out of your body and off of your mind so they no longer drain your energy.

ENERGY LEAK: UNSPOKEN CONVERSATIONS

If you've ever held onto something you wished you had said, you know how much energy it takes to keep it bottled up. Unspoken words weigh on your mind and can negatively affect your relationships. Use the steps on the next pages to help you with the conversation.

Tip: Prior to starting the conversation I would write out your answers to the steps, so you are clear when it is time to speak. Ask the listener if now would be a good time to bring something up or would they prefer to set up a different time later.

1. **Ask the listener to truly listen all the way through without interruption and listen to understand, not to respond.** Listening to respond means focusing on what you want to say next—mentally rehearsing your reply while the other person is still talking. It often comes from a mindset of fixing, debating, or proving a point. In contrast, listening to understand involves giving your full presence with the intent to truly grasp the speaker's thoughts, feelings, or experience.

2. **State the problem you are having as a fact—not a story what was the event that occurred, a one liner.** Facts are neutral and create space for inquiry. Stories are subjective and often trigger defensiveness or reactivity.

Fact	Story
You arrived at 10:15 a.m.	You are always late and clearly don't respect my time.
We have not closed a sale in 30 days.	Our team is falling apart, and no one is doing their job.
She didn't return my call.	She must be mad at me or doesn't care about this project.

You can shift from story to fact by pausing and asking what actually happened (what was seen, heard, or said) and separating the event from your emotion or interpretation.

3. **Tell the listener how you felt.** Name the emotion (I felt angry, sad, frustrated, irritated, etc.).

4. **Tell the listener the thoughts you have about the issue.** This is where you can tell your thoughts as a story referred to above. (Example: I thought that you do not respect my time.)

5. **Tell the listener what you most want.** State clearly what you want. (Example: What I most want is for you to show up on time to our planned meeting times.)

Consider this example of your portion of the conversation, using the above steps, with a teammate at work that missed a deadline:

> Thanks for taking the time to talk. I am sharing this information with you because I value our relationship. Before I share, I'd like to ask you to listen all the way through without interrupting. Please listen to understand, not to respond. That means not mentally rehearsing your reply or thinking about how to fix it—but instead, being fully present to what I'm feeling and experiencing. The deadline for your portion of the project passed on Friday, and it wasn't submitted. When I saw that it hadn't come in, I felt frustrated and a bit anxious. I had the thought that I'm the only one really prioritizing this project right now, and I started to worry that I might not be able to count on you in critical moments. What I most want is to feel like we're both fully committed and can rely on each other to meet our deadlines. That kind of trust is really important to me as we keep working together.

It's important to have these types of conversations in a neutral, calm moment—not in the heat of frustration. Approaching someone when emotions are high often turns a conversation into a conflict, making it harder to express yourself clearly and creating unnecessary tension.

PERSONAL STORY

I learned this firsthand with my son, after many "conversations" that were more like arguments about getting out of bed on time. I had tried everything, and nothing seemed to work. The daily struggle was causing me intense stress every single morning.

One evening at dinner, during a peaceful moment, I decided to approach the issue using the steps. I said, "Please listen without interrupting me. The situation of you not getting out of bed on time is so frustrating to me, and I'm tired of being angry about it. I don't think it's healthy for me to start my day this stressed, and it makes me feel like you don't respect me. What I most want is for you to take responsibility for getting yourself up on time—and if you don't, the consequences will be yours."

We then worked together to brainstorm ways he could take ownership of his mornings. I made it clear that I would no longer be responsible for waking him up, and that if he was late, he'd have to manage the consequences himself. Letting go of that responsibility was hard. I had to work through thoughts like, "What will people think if he's late?" and, "What does this say about me as a mom?" And yes—he was late, many times. Some days he had to take an Uber because I'd already left for work, and other days, he missed school entirely. But over time, it shifted. He now gets up on time, and I finally have stress-free mornings. No more energy leaks on this topic—and that's been a huge win for both of us.

ENERGY LEAK: DOING THINGS YOU DISLIKE

You don't have to do everything—and you shouldn't. One of the most powerful ways to protect your energy is to delegate the things you dislike to people who actually enjoy them. Just because you can do something doesn't mean you should. Even if you're not the boss, that's not a barrier—find a teammate who enjoys the tasks that drain you and look for ways to trade responsibilities. The same applies at home. Consider outsourcing what wears you down, whether it's cleaning, meal prep, or errands. Often, a small investment in support can free up a massive amount of mental and emotional energy. The key is this: spend your energy on what truly matters to you. That's where fulfillment—and freedom—live.

EXERCISE: RECLAIM YOUR "NO"
— Say Yes to What Matters

Objective:

To build awareness of your over-commitment patterns and create the confidence and language to say "no" with clarity and grace.

Step 1: Identify Your "Yes" Triggers

Reflect on the last 3–5 times you said "yes" when you really wanted to say "no." Write them down.

For each one, ask yourself:

- What was I afraid would happen if I said no?
- What did I sacrifice by saying yes?
- What would I have preferred to do instead?

Example: I said yes to helping a friend move even though I was exhausted. I was afraid of seeming selfish. I sacrificed my rest. I would have preferred to recharge at home.

Step 2: Create Your "No" Compass

Clarify your core values or priorities right now. These will become your filter for commitments.

Prompt:

"What matters most to me in this season of life?"

Examples: Health, family time, growing my business, rest, focus, creativity, boundaries.

Step 3: Practice Your "Graceful No" Scripts

Write 3 go-to ways to say "no" kindly but firmly. Practice them out loud until they feel natural.

Examples:
- "I appreciate the ask, but I need to pass so I can stay aligned with my priorities."
- "That sounds great, but I'm over capacity right now and want to honor my commitments."
- "Thanks for thinking of me! I'm learning to not overcommit, so I'm going to say no this time."

Step 4: Build a Pause Habit

When you're asked to do something, pause before responding.

Try this line:

"Let me check my schedule and get back to you."

This gives you time to evaluate if the request aligns with your values and energy.

Step 5: Track Your Progress

For the next 7 days, track:

- When you said no (even small ones)
- How it felt
- What it protected or created space for

Celebrate each "no" as a win. You're creating space for your true "yes."

EXERCISE:
DREAM BIG! WHAT IF NOTHING STOOD IN YOUR WAY?

If you suddenly had unlimited money, freedom, and resources, what would your life look like?

Write this out in full detail—no limits, no practicality, just raw desires.

- What time would you wake up?
- Where would you work (or would you work at all)?
- Who would you spend your time with?
- What would you eat?
- What would your evenings look like?

The more specific, the better.

_____
_____
_____
_____
_____
_____
_____
_____
_____

Now that you have a picture of what life would look like, how can you make at least one aspect a reality?

MY PERSONAL EXAMPLE OF THE DREAM BIG EXERCISE

In 2010, I did this exercise. One thing I wrote: *"I want a full-time cook and housekeeper, so I never have to clean, do dishes, or laundry again."*

I couldn't afford that. But I got creative—I hired someone for two hours a day, Monday through Friday, for $10 an hour (more per hour now). Worth the sacrifice of one dinner out per week. That meant I never had to clean up, prep food, or do laundry, and I eliminated a major energy drain from my life.

Now, 15 years later, I still haven't done laundry.

Protect your energy like your most valuable resource because it is. Change starts one small step at a time. Your energy is precious—spend it wisely.

JOURNAL PROMPT

Reflect on the following questions:

- Where can you close energy leaks in your life?
- What small shift can you make today to protect your energy?

HOW DO YOU WANT TO SHOW UP IN THE WORLD?

Each day, the sun shows up—not rushed, not apologetic, not trying to be the moon. It rises in its full presence, lighting up everything around it just by being what it is.

Event + Response = Outcome

Life is full of unexpected events, some small, some life-changing. You can't control what happens to you, but you can control how you respond. Your response is what shapes the outcome.

THE POWER OF THE SPACE BETWEEN EVENT AND RESPONSE

Viktor Frankl, a Holocaust survivor and psychologist, once said:

> *"Between stimulus and response, there is a space. In that space is our power to choose our response. In our response lies our growth and our freedom."*

The more space you create between an event and your response, the more power you have over your life. But here's the challenge: most of us have automatic reactions—ingrained habits built over years. Our brains create deep grooves that make us respond in the same way to familiar triggers. Unless we interrupt the pattern, we'll keep reacting the same way.

The hardest part of this change is catching yourself before you react. Here are tools to help:

INSTANT STRATEGIES TO EXTEND YOUR RESPONSE TIME

- The 5-Second Rule — Count to five before reacting.
- The STOP Method:

  - Stop.
  - Take a deep breath.
  - Observe your body, emotions, and thoughts.
  - Proceed with awareness.

- **Take a Break** — Walk away, get fresh air, or physically remove yourself.
- **Anchor Yourself** — Press your fingertips together, touch an object (ring, bracelet, etc.), or hold something grounding.
- **Ask Yourself Powerful Questions** — *Is this worth my energy? What story am I telling myself right now? How would my best-self respond?*
- **Use Mantras** — *"Pause. Breathe. Choose." "I am in control of my response."*
- Have a Go-to Response Instead of Reacting:

  - "Let me think about that."
  - "I hear you. Let's talk in a bit."
  - "I need a moment to process this."

Sometimes, the best response is no response at all. When we're triggered, our nervous system automatically shifts into fight-or-flight mode—and that's not the state you want to respond from. In those moments, your body is flooded with adrenaline, your judgment becomes clouded, and emotional reactions can feel urgent or necessary. But the truth is, they usually aren't.

If you notice yourself in that reactive state, pause. Don't respond right away. Instead, take a step back, breathe deeply, and give your body time to calm down. Once your nervous system has settled and your mind is clear, you'll be able to respond from a place of intention rather than emotion. Your calm response will always be more powerful than your reactive one.

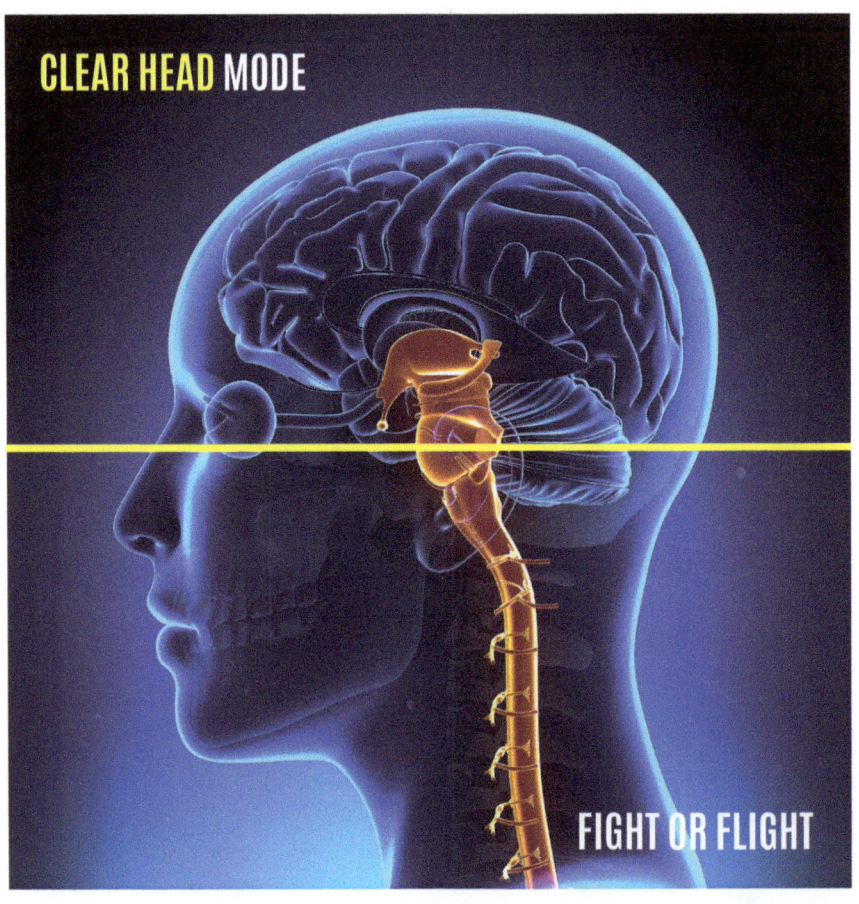

Breaking old reaction patterns is a process and, like any meaningful change, it takes time. You need to practice self-compassion along the way. You won't get it right every time (and that is okay). You will make mistakes—that's not failure, it's growth in motion. What truly matters is how you respond to those moments. When you slip up or react impulsively, forgive yourself and choose to learn from it instead of dwelling on it. At the same time, don't overlook your progress. Celebrate the small wins—like the times you paused, took a breath, and responded with intention. These moments add up. The more you reflect on how good it feels to respond from awareness rather than impulse, the more you reinforce those positive changes moving forward. Self-compassion isn't a soft excuse, it's the strong foundation that makes lasting growth possible.

PERSONAL STORY

My personal struggle with showing up in ways that didn't align with my values—especially my values as a parent—has been one of the hardest parts of my journey. My youngest son, who I love deeply, has a unique ability to push my buttons. I've had many triggers around him, and for a long time, I reacted to those triggers in ways I'm not proud of. I would yell—sometimes sounding like someone I didn't even recognize. I'd be embarrassed if anyone overheard me. Afterward, the guilt would hit hard. I'd feel like the worst mom in the world, apologize, and promise myself I'd do better. But unfortunately, the damage was already done.

You've probably heard the saying, *"Sticks and stones may break my bones, but words can never hurt me."* That couldn't be more untrue. Words do hurt—and they linger, especially when spoken in anger.

I found myself stuck in a painful loop, repeating the same pattern over and over. I honestly wondered if I'd ever be able to change because I kept failing. Sometimes I caught myself in time. But many times, I didn't. And yet, I didn't give up.

I kept practicing the very strategies I'm sharing with you in this book. And while it felt like it took forever, I can now say that 90% of the time, I respond with intention instead of reacting from old patterns. It's not perfect—but it's real, and it's progress. If I can break the cycle, so can you.

To truly break old habits and rewire your reactions, it's important to adopt consistent, long-term strategies that reinforce new neural pathways. Visualization is a powerful tool—by mentally rehearsing how you want to respond in challenging situations, you prepare your brain to act with intention. Practicing box breathing* during both calm and stressful moments this breathing technique helps regulate your nervous system and build emotional resilience. Regular meditation and mindfulness further strengthen your ability to stay grounded and present, reducing impulsive reactions. Finally, setting daily intentions each morning—such as, "Today, I will respond with patience," or "I choose calm over reaction"—helps anchor your mindset and align your actions with your values. These daily practices, when done consistently, create the foundation for lasting, conscious change.

*Inhaling for four seconds, holding for four, exhaling for four, and holding again for four.

EXERCISE: REWRITING YOUR TRIGGER RESPONSE

1. **Write down your triggers.**

    · What situations or behaviors make you react emotionally?

    _____
    _____
    _____
    _____

2. **Identify your auto-response.**

    · What do you normally do? (Snap? Withdraw? Get defensive?)

    _____
    _____
    _____
    _____

3. **Ask yourself: Is this the way I want to respond? Will this response get me the outcome I desire?**

    _____
    _____
    _____
    _____

4. Rewrite the response you WANT to have.

- What response aligns with your values?

_____
_____
_____
_____

- How will this new response help you achieve the outcome you desire?

_____
_____
_____
_____

By practicing this, you shift from reacting out of habit to responding with intention.

WHAT REALLY MATTERS? ONLY YOU KNOW

In a dense forest, not every path leads to the right destination. You must clear the brush and carve your own way.

Most people move through life in a reactive state—chasing goals, meeting expectations, and doing what they think they should do. Rarely do we pause long enough to ask the deeper question: What truly matters to me? Not what our family thinks. Not what society pushes. Not what advertising tells us. Not what our friends expect. Just us—our truth, our values, our inner compass. The challenge is, most of us have never taken the time or created the space to truly figure that out. We're so busy keeping up with life that we forget to check in with ourselves and ask: *Is this really what I want?*

How do you know what matters to you? Your body will tell you. Our bodies are constantly communicating with us, it's just a matter of learning to listen. One of the clearest signals that you're aligned with what truly matters is the sensation of a Whole Body Yes—when your head, heart, and gut are all in agreement. This internal harmony is how you know you're on the right path, making decisions that align with your values and truth.

To tune into this guidance system, you need two things: awareness in the moment and intentional quiet time. Start by noticing how your body responds to different situations throughout the day. Are you energized or drained? At ease or tense? Then, set aside time to reflect on what lifted you up and what pulled you down. The more you practice this, the clearer your internal signals will become.

Your body gives off signs all day long. When you're doing something that fulfills you, you might feel a sense of flow—where time seems to disappear—along with bursts of energy, deep focus, and a natural sense of ease. On the flip side, when you're doing something misaligned, you may notice shallow breathing, chest tightness, exhaustion even after rest, headaches, or a deep sense of dread in your gut. You might also find yourself procrastinating, resisting, or simply going through the motions.

The key is to start paying attention. Your body knows what matters most to you—it's just waiting for you to listen.

PERSONAL STORY

For most of my life, I was quick to say yes. If someone asked me to do something, my default response was almost always immediate agreement—whether I truly had the bandwidth or not. I didn't pause, I didn't check in with myself, and I certainly didn't listen to what I now call my Whole Body Yes.

Learning to slow down has been a journey. I'm working really hard to break the habit of giving an automatic yes, and instead giving myself permission to pause. Now, when a request comes my way, I lean on a few go-to phrases:

"Let me check my calendar."
"Let me take a little time to think it over."
"Let me sleep on it and I'll get back to you."

These aren't stall tactics—they're sacred space. Space for me to breathe, to feel, and to check in with my gut, my heart, and my mind. When all of those line up in agreement, that's a Whole Body Yes. Anything less than that is a no, or at the very least, a not yet.

One of the most powerful lessons I've learned about this came from a decision I got wrong. I bought a house for all the wrong reasons. It was an impulse buy—like grabbing something off the rack in the checkout line without even thinking. I didn't take the time to sit with it, to ask how my body felt about it, or to question if it truly aligned with what I wanted or needed at the time. If I had listened for the Whole Body Yes, I would have realized that everything inside me was actually screaming no.

The fallout from that decision was costly—financially, emotionally, and energetically. I lost a lot of money on that house, but more than that, I lost trust in my own decision-making. That experience woke me up. It taught me the price of rushing, and the power of the pause.

Now, when something comes up, I listen for that deep, grounded yes—the kind that comes from alignment, not pressure. Because if it's not a *Whole Body Yes*... it's a no.

EXERCISE: BODY AWARENESS JOURNAL

Every day for seven days, track:

- What activities gave you energy?
- What activities drained you?
- What was your body's response during each?

At the end of the week, look at the patterns. Do more of what fills you up, do less of what drags you down.

EXERCISE: DIGGING DEEPER INTO YOUR "WHY"

If your why isn't strong enough, lasting change will not happen. Reflection is key. Set aside dedicated quiet time to think about what truly matters to you.

Ask Yourself:

- What do I deeply enjoy doing—regardless of money, recognition, or expectations?
- What would I still do even if no one else approved?
- When do I feel the most alive?

Then Ask: WHY Does This Matter to Me?

The why is critical.

If your reason is based on someone else's approval, fear of judgment, social pressure, status, or a desire to prove others wrong—keep digging. These motivations may spark action, but they won't sustain it. Keep searching until your why is rooted in something meaningful to you. A powerful, personal why is what fuels lasting change and fulfillment.

It's Not Selfish—It's Necessary

Some may think, "This sounds selfish." It's not. When you live in alignment with what truly matters to you, you have more energy, joy, and presence for the people around you.

EXERCISE: DISCOVERING WHAT TRULY MATTERS TO YOU

Objective: To identify your authentic core values and non-negotiables—the things that feel most true to who you are, regardless of outside pressure, expectations, or past conditioning.

Step 1: Quiet the Noise

Find a calm, distraction-free space. Take three-to-five deep breaths. Close your eyes and bring your awareness inward. Imagine a version of yourself completely free from obligations, titles, roles, or the need to impress anyone. You are just you.

Step 2: Write Freely and Without Judgement

Journal the answers to the following questions. Write down anything that surfaces—images, words, feelings, or memories. Be detailed.

- Who am I when I feel most like myself?
- Who am I when no one is watching?
- When do I feel most alive, fulfilled, or proud of myself?
- When do I feel out of alignment or like I am betraying myself?
- What recurring themes, passions, or truths keep coming back to me?
- What would I do or care about if no one else knew about it?
- If there were no awards, no praise, no likes, no applause—what would matter deeply to me?

_____
_____
_____
_____
_____
_____
_____
_____
_____
_____
_____
_____

Step 3: Define Your Core Values

From your reflections above, write five-to-seven words or phrases that represent your core values—the guiding principles that feel essential to your sense of meaning and joy.

_____
_____
_____
_____
_____
_____
_____
_____
_____
_____
_____
_____

Now narrow it down to your top three non-negotiables—values you are no longer willing to compromise, even if it's uncomfortable.

_____
_____
_____

Step 4: The Alignment Check

Now ask yourself:

· Where in my life am I fully honoring these values?
· Where am I compromising them—and what is the cost?
· What small change can I make this week to better align with my top values?

Write down one or two changes you're willing to try.

_____
_____
_____
_____
_____
_____
_____
_____
_____
_____
_____
_____
_____
_____

You already know what matters—you just have to listen. It's not about what society, family, friends, or culture tells you should be important. It's about tuning into what genuinely feels right to you. Deep down, your values, desires, and inner knowing have always been there. The challenge is quieting the outside noise long enough to hear your own truth.

Are you ready to listen?

JOURNAL PROMPT

How would I feel if I gave myself full permission to live in alignment with what I know to be true for me?

_____
_____
_____
_____
_____
_____
_____
_____
_____
_____
_____
_____
_____
_____
_____
_____
_____

YOU ALREADY HAVE THE POWER

A volcano appears dormant, but beneath the surface, it holds immense power. Your inner strength is waiting to erupt when you trust it.

Many people spend their lives feeling powerless—stuck in situations they don't like, reacting instead of creating, believing that life just happens to them. But the truth is: you have far more power than you realize. You may not be able to control other people. You may not be able to control every outcome. But you can control your thoughts, your beliefs, and your actions. And that changes everything.

MENTAL, EMOTIONAL, AND PHYSICAL POWER: RECLAIMING WHAT'S ALREADY YOURS

Your thoughts shape your beliefs. Your beliefs influence your actions. And your actions ultimately create your life. As Wayne Dyer famously said, "Change your thoughts, change your life." He was right—when you shift your mindset, you shift your reality. You don't have to be a victim of your thoughts or a prisoner of negativity. You have the power to choose new thoughts, new stories, and new perspectives. The question is: will you?

Equally important is your emotional power—the ability to trust yourself. Your heart already knows what's right for you. But are you listening? Most of us don't. Instead, we override our inner voice out of fear, guilt, or obligation. We say yes when every part of us wants to say no. We prioritize others' opinions over our own knowing. That's where the practice of the Whole Body Yes comes in. When something is right for you, your head, heart, and gut align. When something is wrong, your body will tell you—if you're willing to listen.

Then there's your physical power, the space around you. Your environment directly affects your energy. Clutter creates stress. Chaos drains you. But a space filled with peace, light, and intention lifts your spirit and sharpens your focus. Take a moment to look around. Is your environment helping you grow into the person you want to be, or is it holding you back? A calm, intentional space gives you clarity and the energy to focus on what truly matters.

You are not powerless. You never were. You have control over your thoughts, your beliefs, your reactions (especially when you give yourself space before responding), your energy, and, ultimately, the life you choose to create. The power has always been yours. The question is: Are you ready to own it?

PERSONAL STORY

For as long as I can remember, I've been "Miss Responsible." I took on responsibilities that weren't even mine, often before anyone even asked. This began when I was just five years old, the oldest of three children navigating the emotional turbulence of my parents' divorce. I instinctively stepped into a role of caretaker, problem-solver, and fixer.

As I grew up, that role expanded—friends, coworkers, my husband, my kids—I took on their worries, their chaos, their needs. And because I did it so well, people began to expect it. I rarely asked for help, and I certainly didn't hand off responsibilities to others. Occasionally, I'd hit my breaking point and explode from the weight of it all—but then I'd go right back to carrying it.

Recently, I took a personal development class focused on breaking old patterns. One of the most impactful exercises was writing a resignation letter to a part of yourself you were ready to let go of. I chose to write my letter to "Miss Responsible". It was time to step down from that role.

I shared the letter with a few people close to me—not only to explain the changes they might notice, but to help hold myself accountable. Saying it out loud made it real. And to my surprise, something incredible happened: people around me began stepping up, without me even asking.

One moment that truly struck me involved my ex-husband (I had not shared my letter with him, he had no idea I even wrote it). For years, any time our son got sick on his watch, I'd get a call: What do I do? It was the same routine for six straight years. But not long after I wrote my resignation letter, I got a call—not from him, but from Walgreens, saying my son's prescription was ready. I had no idea he was even sick. Turns out, my ex had taken him to the doctor and handled it all on his own. No questions. No calls. No need for "Miss Responsible".

That moment felt like a victory. I thought, Wow—she's really gone.

Letting go of that identity has been one of the most freeing experiences of my life. It doesn't mean I don't care. It means I'm learning to care in a way that honors both others and myself.

EXERCISE: REWIRE YOUR MIND — TRANSFORM YOUR THOUGHTS, TRANSFORM YOUR LIFE

Objective: To consciously shift negative or limiting thoughts into empowering beliefs, creating a mindset that supports growth, joy, and success.

Begin by observing your thoughts. Take a few minutes to sit quietly and simply notice what's going through your mind. Write down any recurring negative thoughts, self-doubts, or limiting beliefs that come up. For example, you might notice a thought like, "I always procrastinate; I'm just not disciplined enough."

_____
_____
_____
_____
_____
_____
_____

Next, question these thoughts. For each one, write the answers to the following questions: Is this 100% true? Where did I learn this belief? What would I tell a friend if they were thinking this way? Often, you'll realize the thought is not a fact, but rather a belief shaped by past experiences or conditioning.

_____
_____
_____
_____
_____
_____
_____

Then, reframe the thought. Turn it into a neutral or more empowering version. For instance, instead of saying, "I always procrastinate," you could say, "I am learning how to manage my time better." Or instead of, "I'm not good at public speaking," try, "I can improve my speaking skills with practice." Write the reframed thought.

_____
_____
_____
_____
_____
_____

After reframing, look for real-life evidence to support your new belief. Remind yourself of past successes, no matter how small. You might write, "I've completed projects before, so I am capable of taking action." Or, "I've spoken in front of people and survived; I can get better." This helps rewire your brain to see possibilities instead of limitations.

_____
_____
_____
_____
_____
_____

Now it's time to act as if your new belief is already true. Imagine how you would think, feel, and behave if you fully believed this new thought. Write down and then act upon one small step that aligns with it. For example, if your new belief is, "I am becoming more disciplined," you might set a timer for 10 minutes and start a task you've been avoiding.

_____
_____
_____
_____
_____
_____

Finally, reinforce this new belief daily. Write it down and repeat it to yourself each morning. When the old thought returns, consciously replace it with the new one. Keep a journal to track your progress and celebrate small wins along the way. With consistency and intention, your thoughts will begin to support the life you truly want to create.

_____
_____
_____
_____
_____
_____

JOURNAL PROMPT

Write a "future self" letter, from the most confident version of you, imagining yourself six months from now with your goals already ahcieved. Write how you feel, (grateful, fulfilled, happy, joyful). Write it as if it is already a reality.

CREATING SPACE FOR THE LIFE YOU WANT

A cluttered garden can't grow strong plants. We must pull the weeds (mental clutter, distractions) to create space for growth.

THREE TYPES OF SPACE YOU NEED TO CLEAR

Creating the elevated life you desire starts with clearing space—mentally, emotionally, and physically. Without space, there's no room for clarity, creativity, or meaningful change. Let's look at the three essential areas where clutter can block your growth, and how to begin clearing it.

First is mental space. Your mind is constantly flooded with thoughts, decisions, and distractions. When your mental landscape is too cluttered, it becomes almost impossible to focus on what truly matters. Signs of mental clutter include overthinking, feeling overwhelmed, difficulty making decisions, and ruminating on the past or worrying about the future. To create more mental space, try a brain dump—write everything on your mind down on paper. Reduce information overload by unsubscribing from unnecessary emails, unplugging from social media, and building quiet time into your day. Set healthy boundaries by saying no to what drains you. And create stillness through meditation and deep breathing.

Next is emotional space. Unprocessed feelings take up enormous energy. When your heart is weighed down by resentment, regret, or unspoken emotions, it blocks your ability to feel peace, joy, and connection. Signs of emotional clutter include holding onto grudges, feeling stuck in past pain, or avoiding your emotions altogether. The path to clearing emotional space begins by expressing what's been left unsaid—write it out, talk to someone you trust, or seek closure. Practice forgiveness—not for the other person, but for yourself. And most importantly, learn to tune into your emotions rather than push them away; your feelings are valuable signals, not inconveniences.

Finally, physical space plays a larger role than most people realize. Your environment directly affects your energy, productivity, and sense of well-being.

Cluttered or chaotic spaces often leave you feeling drained, uninspired, or stressed. If you frequently feel tired in certain rooms, can't find what you need, or hang on to things "just in case," it may be time to declutter. Start small—one drawer, one shelf, one space at a time. Ask yourself, "Does this add to my life?" If not, let it go. Then, be intentional about what you keep. Make room for what lifts you up and reflects the elevated life you want to live.

Space creates possibility. When you clear the clutter from your mind, heart, and environment, you open the door to new opportunities, deeper relationships, creative ideas, and greater peace and joy. Let's take a closer look at each area and begin making room for what truly matters.

HEAD

According to a study conducted by researchers at Queen's University in Canada, they estimated that the average person experiences approximately 6,200 thoughts per day and most of them are negative. Which thoughts are occupying space in your head? Are they negative or positive? We need to clear out some of those thoughts, to make room for the thoughts that are going to elevate your life.

We can do this by journaling. Take time to journal on the following topics:

- **Brain Dump Journaling** — This is where you set a timer for 2-5 minutes and just write every thought that pops into your head. Just write, it will not make sense, that is okay, you are doing this to make room for new thoughts.

- **Negative Self-talk** — Write out what negative things you notice you are constantly thinking, then write a positive thought you could think that could replace the negative one.

- **Mantras** — What are sayings that bring you energy? Write them down and put them in areas you spend time in daily, so you can read them repeatedly and create new neuropathways.

Practicing journaling and getting these thoughts on paper allows for creativity to flow, to create space for your elevated life.

HEART

Three powerful ways to clear space in the heart are: releasing stuck emotions, healing old wounds, and letting go of regrets. While the process can be uncomfortable, the relief on the other side is worth it. Remember the J-curve of change—true healing often requires a temporary dip before the rise.

Releasing Stuck Emotions

Getting stuck feelings out of your heart requires acknowledging, processing, and releasing them in a way that aligns with your emotional needs. Here are some effective approaches:

Acknowledge and Name the Emotion

- Identify what you're feeling—anger, sadness, fear, regret, etc.
- Accept that it's okay to feel this way; emotions are messages, not enemies.

Express the Emotion

- Write it out: Journaling can help untangle emotions.
- Speak it aloud: Talk to a trusted friend, therapist, or even record yourself.
- Create art: Paint, draw, or use another form of creative expression.
- Move your body: Dance, exercise, or go for a walk to release stored tension.
- Release through breath and meditation
- Practice deep breathing (e.g., inhale for 4 seconds, hold for 4, exhale for 8).
- Try guided meditation or visualization to imagine the emotions leaving your heart.
- Place your hand on your heart and breathe into the discomfort with self-compassion.

Shift the Energy Physically

- Cry if you need to—tears help process emotions.
- Scream into a pillow or punch a punching bag to release anger.
- Take a cold shower or go for a run to reset your nervous system.

Use Symbolic Acts of Release

- Write down your feelings and then burn, rip, or bury the paper as a symbolic release.
- Imagine placing your emotions into a balloon and watching them float away.
- Throw stones into a river, mentally attaching emotions to each one.

Reframe and Redirect

- Challenge negative thoughts and replace them with empowering ones.
- Find gratitude, even for the difficult emotions—they teach and strengthen you.
- Shift focus by doing something that brings you joy (music, nature, helping others).

Get Support

- A trusted friend or therapist can provide perspective.
- Reading books or listening to talks on emotional healing can offer guidance.
- Spiritual practices, prayer, or connecting with nature can help process emotions.

Time and Patience

- Let emotions flow instead of suppressing them.
- Healing is a process—some feelings take longer to release than others.
- Trust that you won't feel this way forever.

HEALING OLD WOUNDS

Old wounds don't always come from traumatic events; they can stem from seemingly simple moments, like being dropped off at preschool as a 3- or 4-year-old and feeling abandoned. As an adult, you understand that you weren't actually being abandoned, but at that age, your brain wasn't developed enough to interpret the situation accurately. You also didn't have the language to express your emotions or the tools to make sense of what was happening. The result? An abandonment wound that, if left unhealed, can quietly influence your thoughts, emotions, and relationships well into adulthood.

EXERCISE: HEALING OLD WOUNDS

Use the prompts below to explore and begin healing emotional wounds that may still be affecting your present. Take your time. Be honest. Be gentle.

Step 1: Acknowledge the Wound

Healing begins with awareness. Suppressed pain doesn't go away. It shows up in your thoughts, reactions, and relationships. Write in your journal the answers to the questions below, as well as anything else that comes up relating to old wounds.

- What is still hurting me?
- When do these emotions surface the most?
- How does this pain affect my daily life or relationships?

Step 2: Feel it Without Fear

Avoiding emotions only intensifies them. When we allow ourselves to feel, we create space for release. Use tools like deep breathing, calming music, or meditation to help you stay present with your emotions.

Give yourself permission to:

- Cry
- Grieve
- Be angry (in healthy, safe ways)

Step 3: Release the Story that's Keeping You Stuck

We often attach painful narratives to old wounds—stories that no longer serve us.

Common stories might be:

- "I'll never be good enough."
- "People always leave me."
- "I can't trust anyone."

Reframing Practice:

- What story have I been telling myself?
- Is this story really true?
- How would I feel if I let this story go?

Write Your New Story:

- "That was painful, but it doesn't define me. I choose to move forward."
- Reflect on what you've learned and how you've grown stronger because of it.

Step 4: Forgive for Your Own Peace

Forgiveness is not about excusing others—it's about releasing yourself from the burden of pain and resentment.

Who (or What) Do You Need to Forgive?

- A person
- Yourself
- A past version of you

Be completely honest. Let it all out—anger, sadness, disappointment, confusion. This part is for your eyes only, so don't hold back.

Answer these prompts in your journal:

- How has this hurt affected me emotionally, mentally, or physically?
- How has it affected my ability to trust, feel safe, or move forward?
- How long have I been carrying this?

After getting it all out on paper, choose one of the following or write your own statement to open space for healing:

- "I release the weight of this pain. I choose peace."
- "I forgive myself for not knowing then what I know now."
- "I forgive you. Not because what you did was okay, but because I no longer want to carry this pain."
- "I choose peace. I choose to free myself."
- "I also forgive myself—for holding onto this, for how I reacted, or for not knowing how to let go sooner."

Step 5: Write A Forgiveness Letter

With the information you obtained by answering the questions in step four write a forgiveness letter to yourself or the person who harmed you. However, do not send it; it is only for your release.

Forgiveness is not a one-time event; it's a practice. You may need to return to this process more than once, and that's okay. Each time, it will feel a little lighter. Trust that healing isn't linear. Some days you'll feel strong. Other days, the pain might resurface. That's not failure—it's simply part of the healing journey. Remind yourself: "I've survived this before. I am healing, even now." Or say, "Every day, I release more and more." These affirmations ground you in progress, even when it feels slow. Celebrate the small wins along the way. Every step forward matters, no matter how small it may seem.

Healing isn't about erasing the past—it's about making peace with it, so it no longer controls your present. Be patient with yourself. You are stronger than you think. Every time you choose love over fear, self-compassion over self-criticism, and joy over guilt, you are healing. Keep going—you've got this!

LETTING GO OF REGRETS

Regret can be a heavy, emotional burden, keeping you stuck in the past and preventing you from fully enjoying the present. But the good news is you can release regret and transform it into wisdom and growth.

EXERCISE: HOW TO RELEASE REGRETS AND MOVE FORWARD

Step 1: Write down what you regret and how it makes you feel. Be honest, but also be kind to yourself.

Step 2: Write the answers to the following questions:

- What can I learn from this?
- How has this experience made me wiser?
- How can I apply this lesson moving forward?

Step 3: Write that you forgive yourself.

Step 4: Release the "what-if" and "should have" mindset. Regret is often fueled by alternative realities—thinking about how things could have been different. The truth is you can't change the past, but you can change how you carry it.

Write your reframed thoughts.

Examples:
- Instead of: "I should have done X," say: "Next time, I will do Y."
- Instead of: "I wasted time," say: "I learned something valuable."

Step 5: Focus on what you can control now, regret keeps you stuck in the past. Shift your energy to what you can do today.

Write down one action you can take now that honors what you've learned?

Examples:

- Reach out to someone you've hurt or lost touch with and offer a sincere apology or reconnection.
- Help someone else facing a similar struggle by offering empathy, mentorship, or simply listening.
- Change a pattern you once regretted repeating—like setting a boundary where you used to say yes when you meant no.

Step 6: Practice Self-Compassion Daily:

- Healing from regret takes time and self-love.
- Talk to yourself like you would a best friend.
- Replace guilt with gratitude for growth.

Regret isn't a punishment; it's a sign that you're growing. Instead of letting it weigh you down, use it as fuel to make better choices and embrace the life you want.

These exercises are like a cleansing process for your soul, making space for positive energy and experiences to enter your life. Not clearing the clutter of your heart can lead to increased stress, anxiety, depression, and even physical health issues. Opening up space in your heart allows for love to fill in, especially self-love. Your most important relationship is with yourself.

PHYSICAL SPACE

Clearing clutter isn't just about tidiness, it's about making space for new energy, fresh opportunities, and a lighter state of mind. When your environment is crowded with things you no longer need, it can feel like you're holding onto the past, leaving little room for growth and new experiences. Letting go of unnecessary items creates clarity: physically, emotionally, and mentally, allowing you to focus on what truly matters.

A cluttered space often mirrors a cluttered mind and heart, making it harder to think clearly, feel at peace, or move forward. Removing old items tied to past emotions or completing unfinished projects can be incredibly freeing. It's not just about getting rid of "stuff," it's about releasing what no longer serves you so you can welcome what does. Whether it's a new opportunity, a fresh perspective, or simply more room to breathe, an open space invites new possibilities into your life.

A few scientific facts:

- A 2010 UCLA study found that cluttered homes increase cortisol levels, making it harder to relax.

- A 2011 study from the Princeton Neuroscience Institute showed that when too many objects compete for attention, cognitive function declines. Keeping a tidy space helps the brain process information more efficiently, leading to better focus and mental clarity.

- An article written in the Harvard Business Review stated research has shown that our physical environments significantly influence our cognition, emotions, and behavior, affecting our decision-making and relationships with others.

- A 2015 study from St. Lawrence University found that people with messy bedrooms take longer to fall asleep and experience poorer rest. This is because clutter signals disorder to the brain, keeping the mind alert and restless at night. Keeping a clean bedroom fosters relaxation and better sleep quality.

- A 2017 Cornell University study found that people in cluttered kitchens consumed twice as many unhealthy snacks compared to those in organized spaces.

Techniques and exercises to clear the physical clutter, without feeling overwhelmed:

- Start small: Pick one drawer, shelf, or area at a time.

- Don't start more than one project at a time.

- When is the last time you wore or used it? If you haven't used it in a while, let it go.

- Set a timer to declutter. Spend just 5-15 minutes each day tidying up.

- Adopt the "One In, One Out" rule: For every new item you bring in, remove one.

- Make it fun. Play music and or turn it into a game (like pick a color, then go into a room and decide if you are keeping or releasing everything you see that is that color. If you are keeping it, it must have a home and fill you up.).

- Less is more: Too many objects in your line-of-sight cause distractions.

Ultimately, a clutter-free space leads to a clutter-free mind and heart. Your physical environment directly affects mental and emotional states. Keeping organized creates a sense of peace, productivity, and well-being. By removing unnecessary distractions, you can focus better, feel less stressed, and cultivate a living and working space that supports your best self. Whether it's clearing out a desk, tidying up a kitchen, or creating a more serene bedroom, even small changes can have a profound impact on daily life.

Now that you've cleared space in your head, heart, and physical environment, what positive, elevating things do you want to welcome in?

_____
_____
_____
_____
_____
_____
_____
_____
_____
_____
_____
_____
_____
_____

JOURNAL PROMPT

Reflection: After a few weeks of clearing the clutter from your head, heart, and physical space, write down any changes you notice. (How are you feeling? Lighter, more free, happier, less anxiety, etc.)

_____
_____
_____
_____
_____
_____
_____
_____
_____
_____
_____
_____
_____
_____
_____
_____
_____

THE POWER OF FOCUS: DO LESS, ACHIEVE MORE

An eagle locks onto its prey with laser focus. To achieve your goals, sharpen your vision and block out distractions.

In a world full of distractions, your ability to focus is a true superpower. We're often led to believe that doing more equals being more successful—but that's a myth. In reality, one thing done well and brought to completion is far more powerful than ten things started and left unfinished. When your energy is spread too thin, you end up stuck in a cycle of busyness without meaningful progress. Focus isn't about doing more—it's about finishing what matters most.

The real secret to staying focused isn't just willpower, it's your WHY. Distractions will always be there. Life will keep pulling you in different directions. But when your WHY is strong enough, you'll find a way to stay on track. When your WHY is weak, distractions will win every time. On the days when things feel hard, when your motivation is low or time is tight, your WHY is what carries you forward.

Ask yourself: *Why does this matter to me?* If your answer doesn't light a fire inside you, go deeper. When you're connected to a reason that truly matters, focus stops being a struggle—and starts becoming a source of power.

TAMING THE MONKEY MIND: ELIMINATING DISTRACTIONS

Your brain can often feel like a wild monkey—leaping from one thought to another, chasing shiny objects, and reacting to every little distraction that comes your way. This constant mental noise makes it hard to focus on what truly matters. Common focus killers include things like nonstop notifications, multitasking, endless to-do lists, and jumping from one idea or task to the next without finishing any of them.

To sharpen your focus, you need to be intentional. Start by eliminating distractions: silence your phone, turn off notifications, and create a clean, organized workspace. Use time blocks, such as 25-minute Pomodoro sessions, (explained on page 86) to train your brain to work in focused sprints. Prioritize deep work—meaningful, high-impact tasks—over busywork that just fills time. And most importantly, protect your mental energy. Not everything or everyone deserves your attention.

Take a moment to ask yourself: *How am I creating my own distractions?* Sometimes, we unconsciously invite distractions as a way to avoid the discomfort that comes with deep focus—especially when we're afraid of failure, overwhelmed by a task, or unsure where to start. If you're constantly chasing new ideas or shifting from one thing to the next, pause and ask yourself: *What am I really avoiding?* The answers can lead you back to clarity—and focus.

HEART FOCUS: ALIGNING YOUR EMOTIONS WITH YOUR PRIORITIES

Your heart already knows what truly matters to you—but are you giving it your full attention? When your emotional focus is scattered, you may find yourself feeling pulled in too many directions, saying yes to things that don't light you up, and struggling to be fully present in the moment. This disconnect creates emotional fatigue and drains your energy, even when you're doing "all the right things."

To strengthen your heart focus, start by listening for your Whole Body Yes—that unmistakable feeling when your head, heart, and gut are all aligned. If you don't feel that alignment, it's worth reconsidering your priorities. Learn to say no without guilt and protect your energy by choosing commitments that deeply fulfill you. Whether you're spending time with loved ones, working, or creating, practice being fully present. Presence is powerful; it turns ordinary moments into meaningful ones.

Ask yourself honestly: *Am I giving my time and energy to what truly matters to me, or am I spreading myself too thin?* Your heart will always tell you the truth. You just have to slow down and listen.

PHYSICAL SPACE FOCUS: DESIGNING AN ENVIRONMENT FOR SUCCESS

Your physical environment plays a powerful role in shaping your mental clarity, emotional energy, and ability to focus. When your space is cluttered or chaotic, it becomes difficult to think clearly or stay on task. You may find yourself distracted by piles of unfinished tasks, uninspired by your surroundings, or constantly pulled away from what you're trying to accomplish.

To create a space that supports your focus, start by decluttering. Remove anything that doesn't align with your goals or contributes to visual noise. Next, designate a dedicated focus zone—a spot where you can work, think, or reflect with minimal interruption. Enhance your environment with visual cues that reinforce clarity and motivation, such as a mantra on the wall, a vision board, or simply a clean, organized surface. Finally, eliminate disruptions as much as possible. If your environment is noisy or overstimulating, take control by using noise-canceling tools, adjusting lighting, or creating a more peaceful atmosphere.

Ask yourself: *Does my space support the person I want to become, or is it holding me back?* The environment you choose to live and work in can either deplete your energy—or elevate it.

Focus Creates Freedom - When you focus, you finish. When you finish, you move forward.

The more disciplined you are with your focus—mentally, emotionally, and physically—the faster you'll get what you truly want. Your thoughts, your heart, and your space should all work together to support your focus.

EXERCISES TO GET AND REMAIN FOCUSED

These exercises will help train your brain to stay present, minimize distractions, and maintain deep focus for extended periods.

1. The 5-4-3-2-1 Grounding Method (For Immediate Focus)

If your mind is scattered, bring yourself to the present moment using your senses:

- 5 things you can see
- 4 things you can touch
- 3 things you can hear
- 2 things you can smell
- 1 thing you can taste

This resets your brain and eliminates mental clutter.

2. The One-Thing Rule (For Task Completion)

- Ask yourself: *What is the ONE most important thing I need to focus on right now?*
- Eliminate all distractions (phone, notifications, extra tabs).
- Set a timer for 25—50 minutes and work ONLY on that task.

This helps you train your brain to focus deeply without multitasking.

3. **The 10-Minute Intention Reset (For Clarity and Commitment)**

    - Before starting your work, write:
        - *What am I working on?*
        - *Why is it important?*
        - *What are my top three action steps?*

    Review this when you feel distracted to realign your focus.

4. **The Pomodoro Technique (For Sustained Focus and Avoiding Burnout) developed by Francesco Cirillo**

    - Work 25–50 minutes intensely on one task.
    - Take a 5-minute break.
    - Repeat for 4 cycles, then take a longer 15–30 minute break.

    This balances focus and mental recovery.

5. **The Distraction Dump (For a Clear Mind)**

    - Keep a notebook nearby.
    - Whenever a distracting thought arises, write it down and return to work.

    This allows your mind to release it without derailing your focus.

6. The Mental Reset Walk (For Overcoming Mental Fatigue)

    - If you feel stuck, take a 5-10 minute walk WITHOUT your phone.
    - Breathe deeply and focus on your surroundings.

    This refreshes your brain and brings clarity when you return.

7. Focus Training with Deep Breathing (For Instant Re-centering)

    - Inhale for 4 seconds, hold for 4 seconds, exhale for 6 seconds.
    - Repeat for 1-2 minutes whenever you feel overwhelmed.

    This calms your nervous system and sharpens your concentration.

PERSONAL STORY

I used to wear multitasking like a badge of honor, believing it was the secret to getting ahead. I thought the more I could juggle, the more I would accomplish. But the truth? That scattered thinking only stole my peace, slowed my progress, and diluted my power. I'd be knee-deep in one task, already thinking I should be doing something else. It kept me anxious, unfocused, and always feeling behind. Once I learned to harness the power of focused work—and gave myself permission to be fully present—I started to get more done with less stress and greater ease. Now, I choose presence over pressure, and purpose over busy. My productivity flows from clarity, not chaos. That shift changed everything.

JOURNAL PROMPT

Set a 10-minute timer and write down everything on your mind. Then, choose the one thing that is most important today and make a plan to complete it.

ENERGY FLOW: WORKING WITH YOUR NATURAL RHYTHM

A river doesn't fight against rocks—it flows around them. When you stop resisting and align with your natural rhythm, you move effortlessly.

PEACEFUL PRODUCTION: WORKING WITH YOUR ENERGY INSTEAD OF AGAINST IT

We've been conditioned to believe that success requires constant pushing, grinding, and forcing productivity—no matter how exhausted we feel. But real, sustainable productivity—what I call Peaceful Production—comes from honoring your natural energy and working with it, not fighting against it. It begins with trusting the process and staying focused on what's right in front of you. When you commit to a project, stay the course. Don't second-guess yourself halfway through, and don't let your brain convince you that something else is suddenly more important.

Constantly switching tasks or telling yourself, *"I have too much to do and not enough time,"* only keeps you feeling overwhelmed. The truth is, you likely have more time than you realize—it's just about how you're spending it.

Trying a time inventory for one week will help provide clarity. Track how you actually spend your hours—how much time goes toward TV, social media, or distractions, and how much is spent on things that genuinely fill you up versus those that drain you. What you measure, you can manage. Don't rely on your feelings about time; they're unreliable. Ten minutes can feel like forever when you're stuck in traffic or waiting in line, but it can vanish in an instant when you're doing something meaningful or saying goodbye to someone you love. I suggest tracking your time for a week, in half hour increments, to get the full perspective. As a bonus, ask if each task/activity filled you up. I have done this exercise many times, it is tedious, but well worth the effort.

DAY OF THE WEEK:		
Time	Task/Activity	Did task fill you up?
6:00		
6:30		
7:00		
7:30		
8:00		
8:30		
9:00		
9:30		
10:00		
10:30		
11:00		
11:30		
12:00		
12:30		
1:00		
1:30		
2:00		
2:30		

3:00		
3:30		
4:00		
4:30		
5:00		
5:30		
6:00		
6:30		
7:00		
7:30		
8:00		
8:30		
9:00		
9:30		
10:00		

Now imagine if you swapped just 10% of your time spent on low-value activities like social media and tv watching with something that brings personal fulfillment. How different could your life be in six months—or even just one month?

The key to Peaceful Production is to work with your energy, not against it. When inspiration strikes, ride that wave. Dive in, give it your all, and get as much done as possible while the energy is high. But when your energy fades, don't push through it. Take a break—one that truly recharges you. Whether it's a walk, deep breathing, music, or a quick nap, choose what works for *you*. When you push past your limits, quality suffers, burnout creeps in, and the process becomes a grind instead of a flow. Productivity doesn't have to be painful. With the right rhythm, it can be peaceful—and powerful.

Some people might worry that if they stop pushing themselves, they'll never get anything done. Thoughts like, *"What if I never feel 'in flow'?"* or *"I might lose my job,"* or even *"What if I never get off the couch?"* can trigger fear and resistance. But there's an important distinction to make, honoring your energy flow is not the same as procrastination.

Working with your energy means tuning in, knowing when to lean in and when to rest, and trusting that your motivation will return—often stronger—when you allow space for renewal. Procrastination, on the other hand, is avoiding action due to fear, self-doubt, or resistance. One is intentional and aligned; the other is avoidance. The key is learning to recognize the difference and develop awareness around what your body and mind truly need in the moment.

ENERGY FLOW VS. PROCRASTINATION	
Energy Flow	Procrastination
• Work when energy is high, rest when it dips, and return refreshed	• Tasks are avoided out of fear, self-doubt, or resistance
• Work feels aligned and effortless	• Time is spent on doing meaningless things instead of starting purposeful work
• Tasks are worked on efficiently, when inspiration strikes	• Distractions win and casue scrambling at the last minute

When you work in flow, tasks take less energy and get done faster.

THE MAGNET ANALOGY: FLOW VS. FORCE

Trying to be productive when you're out of alignment is like pushing two magnets together on the wrong side—they resist, repel, and frustrate every effort. It feels exhausting and inefficient, no matter how hard you try. But flip one magnet around, and they snap together effortlessly. The same is true for your energy and productivity. When you work with your natural energy flow, tasks come together more smoothly, ideas align, and momentum builds. When you force yourself to push through despite feeling depleted or misaligned, everything takes longer, feels heavier, and leaves you drained. Flow creates ease. Force creates resistance. The difference is everything.

I have many examples of how working with my energy flow has transformed the way I operate. In fact, my daily mantra is Peaceful Production. One moment that stands out was a night when I needed to complete agendas for three meetings I was having the next morning with my executive team. I sat at my desk, trying to force ideas, but nothing inspiring was coming to me. I was tired, drained, and pushing myself to power through.

Instead of continuing to struggle, I made the decision to go to bed and trust that I could finish them in the morning. I'll admit, I was a little worried that the stress of leaving something undone would keep me up all night—but I chose to let the fear go and focus on getting a good night's sleep.

The next morning, something amazing happened. I woke up clear, energized, and inspired. Within just ten minutes, I had written all three agendas—and they were better than anything I could've forced the night before. The ideas flowed effortlessly. Looking back, I know that if I had pushed myself to finish them the night before, it would've taken much longer and the results wouldn't have been nearly as good. This experience reminded me: working in flow isn't just more peaceful—it's more productive, too.

THE HIDDEN COST OF PUSHING TOO HARD

When you constantly force yourself to work outside of your natural energy flow, the cost adds up—quickly. You end up needing longer recovery times, wasting more hours than if you had simply taken a short intentional break. If you keep pushing, eventually, your body will force you to stop. Whether it shows up as sickness, exhaustion, or full-blown burnout, your body always keeps the score. Unfortunately, I learned this the hard way.

PERSONAL STORY

In 2013, I was diagnosed with Non-Hodgkin's Lymphoma and spent the next two and a half years in treatment. You'd think that experience would have been enough to teach me to slow down—but it wasn't. I returned to life and business still pushing myself far too hard. Then, in 2021, I became seriously ill again. The symptoms were intense, but the answers were elusive.

It wasn't until 2024 that I finally received a diagnosis: Common Variable Immunodeficiency (CVID) with Small Intestine Enteropathy. In simple terms, I have no functioning immune system, and my small intestines don't absorb nutrients properly. My body was completely breaking down—and this time, I couldn't ignore it.

Even now, I'm still managing complications and fine-tuning medications. But here's the most important part: I finally learned to honor my energy. I no longer force things. I work in Peaceful Production. I rest before my body demands it. And because of that, my life is more sustainable, more fulfilling, and more aligned than ever before.

HOW TO WORK IN ENERGY FLOW AND ACHIEVE MORE

- **Track Your Energy Levels** — Notice when you feel most productive and schedule your hardest tasks for those times.
- **Follow Your Energy Surges** — When you feel motivation hit, dive in and work hard.
- **Take Intentional Breaks** — Step away when energy dips and do something that truly restores you.
- **Know the Difference Between Flow and Procrastination** — Be honest about whether you're waiting for alignment or avoiding something out of fear.
- **Trust That You'll Get It Done** — When you're in flow, tasks take a fraction of the time compared to when you force them.

The path of least resistance doesn't mean achieving less—it means working in alignment with your energy. When you're in flow, everything feels lighter, more focused, and surprisingly productive. You get more done with less effort, and the results are often better than if you had forced your way through. On the other hand, when you constantly push and force productivity, you create resistance. That resistance leads to struggle, burnout, and longer recovery times that ultimately slow you down. The truth is, you get further, faster—and feel better doing it—when you choose to align with your energy rather than fight against it. So, ask yourself: Which path will you choose?

JOURNAL PROMPT

- Write about a time when you were in flow, fully engaged, focused, and energized?

- What were you doing? What did it feel like in your body? What allowed that flow to happen?

_____
_____
_____
_____
_____
_____
_____
_____
_____
_____
_____
_____
_____
_____
_____
_____
_____
_____

GIVING FROM ABUNDANCE: THE ART OF TRUE GENEROSITY

A well-rooted fruit tree doesn't strain to give—it simply overflows with fruit, season after season, because it's deeply nourished. It draws from rich soil, sunlight, and water, giving from its overflow, not its reserves. When you care for yourself, mind, body, and soul—your giving becomes effortless and sustainable. You won't be left empty, because you're giving from fullness, not sacrifice.

Most of us were taught that giving is good—and that being *selfish* is bad. But what if we redefined selfish as self-nurturing? What if the most powerful and sustainable way to give was to make sure you're full first? Giving should never leave you feeling depleted. If you give without replenishing, it's like trying to breathe out without ever breathing in—eventually, you suffocate. The same is true for giving and receiving; both must exist in balance for true well-being.

When you give without restoring yourself, problems inevitably arise. You become exhausted, resentful, or burned out. Your relationships start to suffer because the giving feels strained or obligatory. You may feel unappreciated, taken advantage of, or emotionally drained. Even the person receiving your gift can sense this depletion, making your generosity feel heavy rather than joyful. This kind of giving isn't sustainable—for you or for those around you.

Now, imagine a different approach: giving from abundance. Picture yourself filled up—mentally, emotionally, and physically—so much so that your energy and joy naturally spill over. Instead of giving from scarcity, you give from overflow. This kind of giving feels effortless, because you are already full. It eliminates resentment, because you're not sacrificing yourself to support others. And it creates a cycle of joy, where giving and receiving both feel good.

The difference is tangible. When you give from abundance, the people around you feel the purity, the intention, and the care behind your generosity. It isn't weighed down by guilt, pressure, or fatigue. It's light. It's clean. It's powerful. And most importantly, it's sustainable. When you take care of yourself first, your giving becomes a true gift—to others and to yourself.

PERSONAL STORY

The way I allow myself to give from abundance starts every morning. My mornings are sacred—they belong to me. I've learned to guard them fiercely, saying no to early meetings, commitments, or even well-meaning friends and family who want to fill that time. It didn't happen overnight. At first, I'd stick to my morning routine for a week or two before letting outside obligations creep in. But over time, I got better—better at planning, better at honoring my needs, and better at letting go of the guilt that came with saying no.

After years of practice, I can now proudly say that 80% of my mornings are mine. I wake up without an alarm, stretch, breathe, journal, color, and enjoy breakfast—completely present. This morning ritual doesn't just ground me—it fills me up so I can give to others from a place of peace, energy, and joy, not from depletion or resentment. It's my daily act of self-respect, and it fuels everything else I do.

HOW TO CREATE ABUNDANCE SO YOU CAN GIVE FREELY

To give from abundance, you first need to achieve abundance.

That means understanding what truly fills you up. And let's be clear, numbing yourself with TV, shopping, drinking, or distractions will NOT fill your soul.

True abundance comes from intentional self-nourishment—from activities that make you feel alive, whole, and at peace.

Here are some examples, but only you can find what works for YOU:

- **Rest** — Taking naps, getting good sleep
- **Body Care** — Massage, yoga, exercise
- **Mindfulness** — Meditation, breathing exercises, journaling
- **Connection** — Talking to someone who lifts you up
- **Nature** — Walking outside, feeling the sun on your skin
- **Creativity** — Reading, painting, puzzles, writing

Some people need more self-care, some need less. The key is consistency.

At first, it may feel like this takes a lot of time. But once your body, heart, and mind get used to it, you will need less time to stay full—just like muscle memory allows an athlete to regain strength quickly after taking a break.

If you keep pouring from an empty cup, eventually, you will have nothing left to give. But when you fill yourself first, giving becomes easy, natural, and joyful. So, ask yourself: Are you giving from depletion or abundance? And if it's depletion, what can you do today to fill yourself up first?

JOURNAL PROMPT

Write a list of things that fill you up and add at least one item from the list to your daily calendar. Schedule time in your calendar and make you a priority, so you can give to your loved ones freely.

_____
_____
_____
_____
_____

YOU FIND WHAT YOU'RE LOOKING FOR

We are lanterns in the dark; what we shine on,

we bring to life.

My personal motto is: "Everything always works out for me." It's more than a phrase—it's a mindset I actively practice. I train myself to notice all the ways life is working in my favor, both big and small. To reinforce this mindset, I keep a running list in the notes app on my phone, documenting each moment where something aligned, resolved, or unfolded better than expected. The key is simple: what you focus on expands. If you look for negativity, you'll always find it. But if you look for the ways life is supporting you, those moments begin to show up more often—and more clearly.

I call it my "It Worked Out" list. It's different from a gratitude list. While gratitude lists help you appreciate what is, this list helps you recognize how things are falling into place—even when it doesn't seem that way at first. Start by writing down everything that works out for you, no matter how small. Pay special attention to the moments that follow something you initially perceived as "bad." Often, those setbacks are actually setups for something better.

Time and time again, I've seen this play out in my life. The delays, the rejections, the disappointments—they've often led to something greater, something I couldn't have planned myself. It might not happen immediately, but in hindsight, it becomes clear. What I have now wouldn't have happened without what came before.

One of my favorite illustrations of this is in the movie *Under the Tuscan Sun*. Frances Mayes goes to Italy after a painful divorce, searching for a fresh start. She dreams of love, family, and a beautiful home—but what she finds is loneliness, uncertainty, and change she didn't ask for. Yet, by the end of the story, a friend gently points out that she did get everything she wished for—just not in the way she imagined. Her life was rebuilt with warmth, friendships, and purpose. She didn't find love in the traditional sense, but she created something even richer.

That story reminds me that when one door closes, another often opens. And sometimes it's not even a door—it's a window, a path, or an entirely different landscape. You just have to be open enough to see it.

So today, I invite you to start your own "It Worked Out" list. Begin noticing the small alignments, the subtle wins, the delayed "no" that became the perfect "yes." The more you pay attention, the more your brain will learn to see opportunity, where it once saw only obstacles. Because truly—everything is always working out for you.

EXERCISE: WHAT ARE YOU LOOKING FOR?

What you focus on, you amplify. If you're always looking for stress, problems, or what's missing—you'll find it everywhere. But if you begin each day looking for peace, kindness, or joy, your mind will start noticing those things more often too.

This journaling worksheet is a powerful way to shift your mindset. It creates awareness of what you've been unconsciously focusing on and helps you choose a more intentional path.

Step 1: Awareness Check

Take a moment to reflect. What have you unconsciously been looking for lately? (Be honest: Fear? Problems? Doubts?)

_____
_____
_____

Now ask yourself: What would I rather be looking for? What would bring more joy, peace, or purpose to my day?

_____
_____

Step 2: Reframe and Redirect

Choose **3 positive things** you want to find more of in your life (use examples below or your own).

- ☐ Joy
- ☐ Peace
- ☐ Beauty
- ☐ Love
- ☐ Magic in the everyday
- ☐ Opportunities
- ☐ Playfulness
- ☐ Kindness
- ☐ Gratitude
- ☐ Connection
- ☐ Other: _____

My 3 Focus Words Today:

1. _____
2. _____
3. _____

Step 3: Spot It and Journal It

Throughout the day, notice when one of your focus words shows up—even in small ways.

Where did I find joy?
Where did peace show up?
When did I feel connection or beauty?

Record them here:

_____
_____
_____
_____
_____
_____
_____
_____
_____
_____

Step 4: End-of-Day Reflection

Take a moment to reflect:

- *How did it feel to look for the positive?*
- *What surprised you?*
- *How did this affect your energy today?*

_____
_____
_____
_____
_____
_____
_____

What are you choosing to look for tomorrow?

_____
_____
_____
_____
_____
_____
_____

THIS ISN'T THE END—IT'S JUST THE BEGINNING

Life is not a mountain to summit—it's a winding river to float down. There's no final peak to conquer, no finish line to cross. The beauty lies in the bends, the ripples, the sparkling moments along the way. Some stretches move fast, others slow, but the point was never to arrive—it was always to enjoy the ride, feel the sun on your face, and notice the dragonflies dancing along the banks

YOU'VE ELEVATED YOUR GREATNESS—NOW KEEP RISING

You've made it to the end of the book—but this is truly just the beginning. Along the way, you've explored what it means to live a life that is free, full, and unapologetically yours. You've uncovered the power of presence, intention, clarity, and alignment. You've examined what's been holding you back, learned how to reclaim your energy, and practiced tuning into what really matters—according to you, not the world around you.

You now know that personal fulfillment is an inside job. It's not about chasing more—it's about creating space for what already lives within you. It's about trusting your energy, following your intuition, and focusing on what fuels you instead of what drains you. You've learned how to work in flow instead of force, how to forgive and release old stories, and how to give from overflow—not depletion.

The tools, exercises, and reflections in this book weren't meant to be followed once and forgotten. They're yours to return to, whenever you need a reset, a reminder, or a renewed sense of direction. Think of it like showering—you can go a day or two without one, but by the third day, you start to stink. It's the same with personal fulfillment. Skip working on yourself for a few days, and life starts to feel a little stale—maybe even *stinky*. Growth is not a straight line. It's a cycle. A rhythm. And your journey will continue to evolve with you.

So, take this truth with you as you move forward, you already have what you need; you are capable, worthy, and powerful. Your job now is to trust yourself, stay awake to what matters, and choose to live on purpose—again and again. Even one small shift can open the door to an entirely new way of living.

MY CHALLENGE TO YOU: SHARE YOUR "aha" MOMENTS

Your insights and breakthroughs don't just benefit you—they inspire others. Share your "aha" moments with friends, family, strangers, or on my website MelissaADotson.com. When you spread positivity, you amplify it—not just in your own life but in the world around you.

So, keep going, keep learning, keep peeling back the layers. This isn't the end. You are the author of what comes next. Keep writing, keep rising, keep living elevated.

BIBLIOGRAPHY

- Beckhard, R., and Harris, R. T. *Organizational Transitions: Managing Complex Change*. Addison-Wesley, 1987.

- Chand, Suma, Daniel P. Kuckel, Martin R. Huecker. "Cognitive Behavior Therapy." Last Update: May 23, 2023. https://www.ncbi.nlm.nih.gov/books/NBK470241/

- Cirillo, Francesco. The Pomodoro Technique. https://www.pomodorotechnique.com/

- McMains, S., and Kastner, S. "Interactions of Top-Down and Bottom-Up Mechanisms in Human Visual Cortex." *The Journal of Neuroscience* (2011): 31(2); 587–597.

- Radin, Rachel, PhD; Aric Prather, PhD; et al., "Digital Meditation to Target Employee Stress" *JAMA Network Open*. January 14, 2025.

- Sander, Libby. "The Case for Finally Cleaning Your Desk." *Harvard Business Review* (March 2019). https://hbr.org/2019/03/the-case-for-finally-cleaning-your-desk

- Saxbe, D. E., and Repetti, R. L. "No Place Like Home: Home Tours Correlate With Daily Patterns of Mood and Cortisol." *Personality and Social Psychology Bulletin* (2010): 36(1), 71–81.

- Thacher PV, Reinheimer A. "Sleep quality and sleep disturbance in those at risk for hoarding disorder." Sleep. June 2015; 38: A325.

- Vartanian, Lenny, Kristin M. Kernan, and Brian Wansink. "Clutter, Chaos, and Overconsumption: The Role of Mind-Set in Stressful and Chaotic Food Environments." *Environment and Behavior* (2016).

ABOUT THE AUTHOR

By the time she turned 18, Melissa Dotson had moved 33 times, an upbringing that fostered her adaptability, gratitude, and the value of perseverance. Those early challenges taught her resilience, fueled her determination, and shaped her into the resourceful leader she is today.

Melissa began her career as a CPA with a Big 4 accounting firm, developing a strong foundation in finance and business operations. In 1998, she joined Rieke Interiors as CFO. Her entrepreneurial drive and passion for learning quickly led her to immerse herself in every facet of the business—from operations to client experience. Her comprehensive understanding of the company, paired with her natural leadership abilities, made her the clear choice to step into the role of President in 2009. A decade later, in 2019, Melissa purchased the business, continuing to lead Rieke Interiors with a unique blend of strategic vision and a people-first philosophy. Under her leadership, the company continues to thrive—balancing profitability with purpose and placing culture at the center of its success.

At the heart of Melissa's leadership philosophy is a commitment to personal fulfillment. She has spent over 20 years studying and practicing personal development, integrating these principles into her life and business. Her team members are not just employees—they are valued individuals whose personal and professional growth is nurtured through programs, like the "15 Commitments to Conscious Leadership," and tools, like the Culture Index.

Melissa is not only a successful CEO but also a passionate advocate for self-awareness and purpose-driven living. Her own life experiences, from overcoming personal obstacles to battling serious health challenges, have deepened her empathy and fueled her determination to help others thrive. She believes that transformation begins with small, consistent steps toward change. Melissa's journey from survival mode to success is a testament to the power of mindset and action. She now focuses on sharing her hard-earned insights through speaking engagements, workshops, and coaching. Melissa's ultimate goal? To inspire individuals and organizations to unlock their potential, embrace their purpose, and elevate their lives to the most fulfilling and impactful version possible.

Outside of her professional endeavors, Melissa is a proud mother of two and a grandmother of two. She finds joy in activities like boating and spending time at the beach—places that ground her and remind her of the beauty in life's simple pleasures. Melissa's life philosophy is summed up in a single phrase: "Everything always works out for me." Through this lens, she turns challenges into opportunities and helps others do the same.